Orlando Property Success

Paula McLaren

Please note!

This book is an ongoing project. Any suggestions you may have to make this book the best I possibly can are very welcome. Remember to register for any updates as you are entitled to free updates for life. Register by sending an email to paula@housebuyorlando.com or by subscribing to the website www.housebuyorlando.com.

CONTENTS

1 INTRODUCTION

I would first of all like to thank you for choosing to buy this book. I hope it gives you all of the information and tools you need to go out and buy **your dream property in Orlando**. If you are a seller of a property then I will also be covering that aspect too.

A few years ago, I was in a similar position to the one you are in now. I wanted to buy a property in Orlando and had no idea how to go about it or what it entailed. It became my dream to live in Orlando after visiting on a work trip. I fell in love with the whole state of Florida, from the Florida Keys, Naples, West Palm Beach, and Clearwater to Orlando itself. I wrote down my goals, implemented my plan and two years later was working and living in Florida. I was 25 years old.

Faced with the prospect of buying a property with no understanding of the correct procedure or property values in the United States, I made a few unnecessary mistakes. Had I been lucky enough to have access to a book like this, I would have saved myself a great deal of time, effort and most importantly money and that is what I aim to do for you.

I built a career in the property market as a real estate professional and after 10 years of helping people buying and selling homes, I now have a huge insight into the ins and outs that you should know before starting the process of buying property in Florida. Much of my working life has been spent providing this information to help my clients achieve their dreams and I hope that I can help you to achieve yours too. In this book, I have put all my knowledge down in one place for you to read, absorb and use as a guide. This is something you can refer to time and time again for your benefit.

Throughout this book, I will be offering you 'Quick Tips'. These will be very important tips on how to save money and time during the property purchasing process. These tips are key areas of the book and you should pay particular attention to these sections. Of course you may want to highlight your own sections, so make sure you have a highlighter pen ready. It will make it easier when you need to go back to refer to specific areas.

I am certain that this book will save you time and money, and should make the process of buying or selling a property in Orlando a much more straightforward one. It really is not complicated at all. Whilst I cannot guarantee that you will make money on any property in the long or short term, (I don't actually have a crystal ball and if I did, my job would be incredibly easy!) What I will do though is make the process as easy as I can and give you all the knowledge you need to be able to do exactly what I did.

It seems like only yesterday that I relaxed beside the pool for the first time watching the amazing Florida wildlife from my pool deck. It was a beautiful, warm day and with a cool drink in my hand, I just sat and reflected on how I had gone from a simple dream to living the reality. **It was an incredible moment that I will never forget and I was lucky enough to spend many years living my dream. This guide will help you to do the same.**

If you are looking for a second home to go to when you want some sunshine and friendly Florida lifestyle, this is the guide you will need. If you are looking for a long term investment property that you can rent out until you either want to use it yourself or want to sell on, this guide will help you do that too.

In this book, I will be revealing everything that the buying process entails. It may be that you have already acquired some information by researching from different sources. However, you will benefit from the extra knowledge that I am making available and even if it is just a few more aspects of the process, it could still save you time and money.

Time and money that you would have otherwise wasted.

Do remember that this book is based upon my knowledge and experience of the property process in Orlando. I will always do my utmost to present the facts that I have learned over the years, in an open and honest fashion. Due to the changing nature of the property market, the content is under constant revision, therefore, if you have a special tip you feel I haven't covered, just let me know and I can include it in my updates.

Buying a property in Orlando is not as difficult as you may think. What I can pass on to you is the experience of going through the process for myself and for hundreds of other buyers and sellers too.

The reason many people go about buying a property in Orlando the wrong way and can lose money doing so is because they don't research the process properly (it is very different to buying property in the UK) and they don't take the right action on the information that is presented to them. It is of course entirely up to you whether you put into practice the information that I am presenting here, however, if you implement just a few of the different tips, it should help you a great deal and the book will pay for itself many times over.

It is also very easy to get caught up in your dream and the emotion of it all. Be very wary of anything that sounds too good to be true, as it usually is the case, although it may equally be worthy of further investigation. Make sure that you are diligent and take professional advice from the right people.

As with any property purchase there is of course some work involved with the buying process. Only you can put in this effort to make it a more worthwhile investment of your time and money. This book can help you with that work and save you hours and even weeks of your time too.

Ok, are you ready to get started? Then let's get down to the detail.

2 YOUR ULTIMATE GOAL

First a question. I want to begin by asking you **what is your ultimate goal for seeking to buy a property in Orlando, Florida.** Really take time to think about this properly. Write your goal down - be very specific!

Is it your goal in life to move to the sunshine state and enjoy a slower paced, more relaxed life and warmer climate? Florida is such a popular destination for retirees and people wanting to live in the sun due to the fantastic lifestyle it offers. There are many flights to and from the UK which can provide visiting friends and relatives with a taste of paradise in less than a day's travel time.

There are also ways of moving permanently to Florida and this can be done through various means. Remember, if this is your goal then you will almost certainly be buying a property based upon emotion, since it will become your family home for the foreseeable future. If buying a home to live in, certain criteria will be paramount to you that would not apply if you were buying a property as an investor looking for income and capital growth.

It might be that you just want a second home in the sun to visit now and again to enjoy the endless possibilities of things to do in Florida. It is possible to keep visiting your home and do completely different things each time. People return to Orlando year after year because there is no language barrier, the weather is fabulous all year round, the restaurants are second to none and the shopping/entertainment are fantastic.

If you are buying a property for your own occasional use and also to rent out in your absence, then it is likely that you will have something of an emotional view on the purchase. When you are enjoying your property you will want certain criteria to be met. Be clear as to what these may be. Do they include, a South/West facing pool; an owners closet to lock away your personal linen/items; close proximity to certain attractions and shops; easy access from the airports; a gated community; a community with facilities such as resort pool, gym, Wi-Fi in the clubhouse, on site cinema, tennis courts etc? You need to discuss your specific requirements with your agent so that you can be assured of having everything you want when you visit your home in the sun.

Lastly, you might be buying a property purely as a long term investment. At the moment, prices are extremely low, in the region of 40% lower than this time seven years ago! A property that cost around $350,000 at that time can now be bought for much less. It can be rented out to cover costs until you decide to sell. For this type of purchase you need to remove any emotional thoughts you might have about what you would want if you lived in the property. **The most important thing is that your chosen property meets the right criteria for renting out.** Remember, without a good rental income you will not be able to service the outgoings on your investment. Don't get caught up in any emotion at all. **Look at it as a business transaction**. Make a list of possible properties and work through the list until you find one that meets all of your criteria. Only then should you consider signing a contract to purchase your chosen property.

3 OWN YOUR DREAM PROPERTY

Just imagine owning a property in the world's number one tourist destination. Imagine visiting that home and enjoying the rewards it will bring. Imagine being able to provide a beautiful experience for your close family or friends. Imagine living the Florida dream. Imagine ticking off another box on your list of life's goals which reads 'own an investment property overseas'.

What I am going to tell you in this book is **how to achieve your dream.** I will be including every minor detail of the process which will enable you to think it through, step by step, put it into practice and comfortably reach the destination you seek.

If you have no experience of buying property in the UK don't worry. The procedure is very different from buying a property in the UK anyway. If you have bought property in the UK, then wipe your mind clean of that experience as the process in Orlando is completely different.

All it will take is a little time and effort for you to reap the rewards of owning a property in Florida.

4 WHY MANY PROPERTY DREAMS FAIL

Firstly people don't seek out the right information beforehand. You are ahead of the crowd by buying this book and following a proven plan

There are many stories that you can find about people who have bought property in Florida the wrong way. Just look online or in the newspapers. You will find forums and articles that can discourage you from taking action because the people concerned did not attempt to seek out the knowledge and do it the right way. During my years of living in Orlando, helping people to fulfill their dream of owning a property, I have met many who took the wrong route because they failed to find out the right way to proceed before committing to buy.

From the moment you step on the plane you will meet someone or see an advertisement which could possibly lure you into buying the wrong property. Make sure you have done your research first. Don't be distracted by offers that sound too good to be true (it means they usually are). Research thoroughly, be diligent and make sure that you have built a good relationship with your agent beforehand and stick with them throughout the process.

Don't allow yourself to be easily parted from

your life savings or cash in your pensions or sell up your life in the UK with the offer of a property in the wrong location that will not rent.

Don't let yourself be sold a business, that is not really a business, to obtain legal status such as a visa. Remember, it is not easy to move to the United States to work, however, it can be done and you must get it right. If you do it the wrong way there could be serious consequences. To avoid possible disappointment and even worse, financial complications, don't try to do it all on your own. **Make sure that you do your research, seek professional help and be diligent.**

A good agent who has been working in the industry for many years will have access to a whole list of professional companies to support you. Solicitors, inspection companies, mortgage brokers, banks, title companies (perform the completion), tax advisors and many more. These are all companies you will need to access in order to make your purchasing process as straight forward as possible.

5 THE IMPORTANCE OF FINDING A REALTOR

This is probably the most important step at the beginning or your property journey.

A Realtor is seen as a US version of an estate agent. There is a huge difference to buying a property in the US compared to the UK and this is probably one of the most important. Find a Realtor who is a member of the National Association of Realtors and Florida Association of Realtors. They also need to be a member of their local Board of Realtors such as OSCAR or ORRA. If they are not members, find one who is.

A good Realtor will assist you with home inspections, pest inspections (surveys), mortgages, valuations (appraisals), opening a bank account, liaising with the title company (similar to a solicitor's role), checking the closing (completion) documents and much, much more. They will be your first point of contact after your purchase for any questions you may have and advice you may need.

Make sure that the Realtor you choose is committed to you in the form of a buyer's agent. This means they will work on your behalf looking through hundreds of properties to find one that meets the parameters that you have set down. They will ask you questions regarding your requirements to make sure they find the best property to suit your needs.

It is a fact that the 80/20 rule works in the property industry in Florida and you may be surprised to know that 20% of agents sell 80% of the properties. Therefore always check how long your agent has been selling property in Florida and make sure they are one of the 20% of agents who work daily in the property industry. An agent who dedicates their time and energy to the property business will have the knowledge and client base which will prove a huge benefit for you.

A good agent will be aware of properties not on the open market that are for sale through their client list and networking efforts. This service alone could save you thousands of pounds and a great deal of time.

When you choose the right agent, nothing will be too much of an effort for them. If you need help with any aspect of owning a Florida property, your agent will be there for you and many people find that their agent becomes a good friend. This special relationship is worth cultivating because, over time, you will need assistance with various different matters and you will be able to call on your agent for advice and assistance.

As with property purchasing anywhere, frustrations can occur. Things can crop up during the purchasing process and sometimes afterwards that can be unsettling, particularly if you are trying to buy a property without professional help. A good agent will take away all the usual stresses and worries completely, by dealing with each query as it arises.

Quick Tip

If you find a property by searching through the internet, contact the agent that is advertising the property and find out if that agent is actually the listing agent for that property.

If that is the case you will need to find your own buyer's agent to deal with your side of the purchase. **A listing agent is working for the seller. Although they can deal with you and the seller, their loyalty lies with the seller**. Remember, if you do decide to let that agent represent you, then do not disclose to them how much you can afford to pay, or are willing to pay, as this gives the negotiating power to the seller. Even though we are in a buyer's market, disclosing your position to a listing agent could cost you thousands of Pounds. **A buyer's agent does not cost you anything. Make sure you have one guiding you through every step of the way.**

6 LOCATION, LOCATION, LOCATION

Always buy on location not on price. There are some spectacularly low prices for properties in Orlando, Florida today. Don't be tempted by adverts and offers which are incredibly low. A $35,000 condo may not be so attractive when you are unable to rent it out because you have bought in the wrong part of town and it is too far away from the main attractions and facilities. Don't be tempted by offers that make you send your deposit immediately as they are selling out fast. There will be plenty of property available and it is worth paying a slightly higher price to source the right property with a good cash flow return on its rental.

Remember, your Realtor will find you the best property, in the best location within your price range. Every price range has better locations included in it. You will need to take advantage of buying as close to the action as possible.

When people rent a property in Florida it is usually to enjoy the climate and visit the attractions and beaches. It is important that there is a supermarket close by for tired families in need of quick provisions after a long journey. If the property is easy to find, in a popular well known location, this will attract renters who are familiar with the area and the facilities available to them. Even more importantly, this will also attract repeat bookings to your property (a great thing!).

Don't forget, you may want to sell your property in the future and it will always be easier if you have bought in the best location possible. Even in the very low priced market we have at the moment, the best locations are being snapped up with multiple bids being made on each property.

Don't be tempted by a house twice the size, but a bit further away from the amenities. A large house means larger utility bills. A larger garden means huge utility bills! It may look like a bargain until you receive your electricity and water bills. Just keeping the property cool and the lawn watered (which has to be done on a daily basis in Florida) will result in very high bills. A smaller house in a better location could make you money! You will achieve more rentals to pay for your overheads which will allow you to enjoy your property as and when you want to.

Quick Tip

Ask your Realtor to check the pending properties (under contract) together with recently sold properties to see if you are paying the correct price. Some of the bank owned properties or short sales are very low in price and can be purchased in the right location too. The range of prices is huge; **make sure you do your research so you are not paying over the odds.**

7 GET YOUR FINANCES READY

Contact a mortgage broker or bank and obtain your pre-qualification and then your pre-approval. Your Realtor should have contacts with mortgage brokers and banks that deal with similar purchases and have experience with foreign investors and second home owners.

Consider also borrowing funds in the UK. It is often easier and more cost effective to release funds from your UK property. Check with your mortgage broker to see if a home equity loan would suit you better. Compare the interest rates with the US mortgage broker or bank before committing yourself.

There are still a few banks lending to foreign investors in the US market and the interest rate is hovering around 6.75%. Although this does seem like a high interest rate compared to UK banks, it may still work better for you to have your mortgage in the US. Your agent will help you assess the best way to move forward and point you in the right direction for a tax advisor to explain the pros and cons also.

Usually you will be required to put down a 30% deposit although a slightly lower deposit may be available.

Quick Tip

It is imperative to **find a mortgage broker who is used to dealing with this type of market**. Residential mortgages are very different to investor mortgages. Dealing with the wrong mortgage broker could be the difference between your purchase completing or losing your property at the last minute because the broker was unaware of the requirements when dealing with foreign investors.

Quick Tip

Always ask your mortgage broker or bank for a good faith estimate at the beginning of your discussions. This is a one or two page document that lists every type of cost that you will incur at the closing/completion stage. It will include items such as property taxes, home-owners association fees and joining costs which will be pro-rated to the date of closing. All of the mortgage broker and bank costs will be listed on the form.

This will enable you to take the time to look through the costs and discuss them with your agent. Imagine getting to the completion table and then being told your costs to purchase the house are going to amount to between 3% and 4% of the cost of the mortgage. Having an estimate of these costs will make sure you can allocate these funds ahead of time and will prevent surprise costs arising at the last minute.

Remember that this good faith estimate is only an estimate. It is not a guarantee of the costs. A good bank or mortgage broker should over-estimate these costs but this is not always the case. I would strongly advise you put aside some extra funds above these estimates for completion (allow $500 approximately). If you don't need them, you can put the extra funds towards getting your home set up for rental instead.

8 OPENING A US BANK ACCOUNT

If you are making a cash purchase, obtain proof of funds, before you make an offer on a property. This could be a straightforward letter from your bank. A seller will not entertain a cash offer without this document. As the prices today are very low, several offers are being made on each property so **it is imperative you have a strong offer** otherwise you could be looking at making offers on several properties without any success at all. A strong offer means that proof of funds, proof of deposit and/or your mortgage offer is included. This is a crucial point for having a good Realtor (estate agent) who will assist with these details.

Make sure that you are well prepared in advance. Contact your bank for a letter to confirm that you have the funds available for your property purchase. Or obtain proof of funds in the form of a bank statement. Make sure that you have this proof before you start to look for a property so that as soon as your agent finds a great property you are able to put forward a written offer. If you have not obtained your proof of funds, this will delay the offer and the house will sell to someone else.

Quick Tip

You will need to open a bank account in the US if you

don't already have one. This can usually be done with the help of your mortgage broker. **Without a US bank account you will not be able to obtain a mortgage.**

You will also need to put some mortgage reserves in this account to show proof of ability to pay the mortgage before completion. This can amount to six months of reserves. Each lender is different. These reserves can be taken out immediately after closing but will need to be transferred to your US bank account as soon as your mortgage broker advises.

It is not difficult to open a US bank account. If you are making a purchasing trip to Florida then you can do this when you arrive. There are certain banks that are used to opening foreign investor accounts where you will find the process easy. There are also banks that never come across this type of client. Your real estate agent will advise you on where to go and what to do.

It may also be possible for the bank providing your mortgage to open an account for you. Again, your real estate agent will advise you of this process.

Even if you are paying cash for the property you will need to set up direct debits for your utilities and other fees. It is easier for you to control and check for errors than giving the responsibility to the management company to pay your bills for you.

Your income from rentals can also be paid into this account. This will make the process of filing taxes, deducting expenses and controlling the investment much easier than trying to do it all from a UK bank account.

NOTES

enquiries@choiceoverseas.
Co.uk.

Tel 0845-260-2144

If you are making a trip to view properties, open your bank account when you get there. You will need your passport and funds for a deposit. Your agent will direct you to the best location to do this.

9 APPLYING FOR A MORTGAGE

This is a straightforward process starting with the first email or telephone call with your mortgage broker. They will ask you questions pertaining to your financial circumstances and will ask you to complete a mortgage application form. The form can be completed and returned via email or fax. Your mortgage broker can then issue your pre-approval notice. This is confirmation that you qualify for a loan and will be used to show the seller of the property that you are a pre-approved buyer.

Quick Tip

Throughout the mortgage process your mortgage broker will be constantly asking for documentation from you. This is basic, standard information, such as bank statements, proof of earnings etc.

Make sure you obtain any requested information quickly and send this to your mortgage broker. Florida real estate contracts adhere to a strict time limit and 'time is of the essence'.

Any delay with requested documents on your part could result in termination of the contract and a loss of your deposit.

Your mortgage broker can give you a list of required documents in advance. Start collating these items immediately. The list will look something like this.

1) Copy of passport.

2) Evidence of a US Bank account.

3) Two months most recent Bank Statements from your UK bank account.

(These statements should be for an account showing your deposit money available)

4). Three reference letters to show you have a good payment record. These letters could be from a bank, credit card company or utility company.

10 MAKING AN OFFER

When you have found a property you want to place an offer on then you need to advise your real estate agent. Your agent will then put the offer in writing for you and you will need to sign it. The offer is written on a standard Florida contract. Verbal offers are very rarely negotiated or accepted.

If you are dealing with a short sale property or a bank owned property then the process will be much longer. Be prepared for a long wait from the bank to make a decision. Bear in mind that the property you are buying may be massively reduced and it will pay to be patient.

11 NEGOTIATING

Following submission of your offer, you will receive either a counter offer from the seller with a different price and possibly terms or the seller will agree and sign your offer.

If the property is being sold on a short sale basis then it will probably be a case of multiple offers being received. This will not give you a chance for negotiation and you must make your best offer to start with. If the property is a seller (vendor) owned property then there may be some room for negotiation.

Your agent will assist you with every aspect of the negotiation process. If you find that you are within a few thousand Dollars of the price you want to pay, don't necessarily walk away from the property. There may be a way that it can work for both parties and your agent will come up with suggestions to make this work for both of you.

12 AGREEING THE PURCHASE

As soon as both parties are in agreement and both have signed the contract then the contract becomes binding. The only "get out" clause would be at the home inspection stage or if your loan is refused.

Time is of the essence from this moment so make sure you adhere to all the requirements made from the seller.

Your agent will assist you with the next steps of the process. Providing you meet all of the requirements as per the contract there should not be a problem from this point. The seller is also bound by the contract from this point.

13 PROPERTY INSPECTION

If this is a seller (vendor) owned property then a home inspection may have been negotiated as part of the contract. This means that a home inspection company will visit the property, inspect every aspect of it, including the roof, air conditioning units, plumbing, pool equipment etc. They will make a full list of items that need repairing. This will be presented to the seller. There is a time frame when this has to be done by so be very careful to follow the contract. Your agent will help you with this.

14 SELLER REPAIRS OR "AS-IS"

The term "as-is", is a commonly used one in the US where property is concerned. It simply means the property is sold as it is seen when viewed by the buyer and an offer is made. The seller does not warrant that anything will work as it should and this is the risk the buyer takes. It is usually common in a seller's market, however, as many of the properties are now in repossession stages this is most often not the case today. Also, if the seller is in negative equity with their property then an as-is sale is most likely as the seller will not have any funds to make repairs to the property.

If the contract is subject to seller repairs, then the seller has the responsibility of repairing the items with a licensed repair company up to the amount stated on the contract. The buyer can then ask the home inspection company to check the repairs (there is usually an additional charge for this).

As the property market has gone through a huge downturn many properties are being sold as-is. This means that the buyer accepts the property as it was when the contract was signed. Under these circumstances, the seller will not make any repairs to the property and the property is sold as seen.

15 PEST INSPECTION

There is also a need for a pest inspection on any properties that are not new. This basically means a termite inspection. Termites are insects, common in Florida. They can eat their way through wood very easily and can cause great damage to a home.

If any damage is found, the pest inspector will note this on the report and you can then present it to the seller. Again, the seller has to make the necessary repairs up to the amount noted on the contract.

The pest inspector will re-visit the property when the repairs are completed to make sure they are done to a satisfactory level.

Your real estate agent will organize all of this for you and liaise with the different inspection companies on your behalf.

16 HOME WARRANTY

When you complete on your home you will have the option of purchasing a home warranty for the property.

This is a comprehensive cover for many things in the home such, as air conditioning units, cooker, pool, roof and other items. This is a very worthwhile investment especially if you will be renting the property when you are not using it.

If something goes wrong then it is simply a case of your management company contacting the home warranty company and a repair person will be sent to the property.

It could save you thousands of pounds in repairs. Ask your agent to give you the details of the different companies available. They will arrange this for you as part of the completion process. **Having a comprehensive home warranty can save you a fortune over the years of owning a property.**

17 HOME INSURANCE

More commonly known as hazard insurance. If you are mortgaging the property you will not be able to complete the purchase without hazard insurance. This is equivalent to buildings insurance in the UK. There are many companies offering this service at a reasonable cost.

There will be an excess on the insurance policy which will be deducted from any claim you may have to make. This is known as a deductible in the US. Again, this is something your mortgage broker or real estate agent can assist you with.

18 THE COMPLETION (CLOSING) IN ATTENDANCE

If you are planning on being present at the completion of your purchase, then you will need to take photo identification with you (passport).

Completion will take place at the title company's office (similar to UK solicitor) which is usually chosen by the seller of the property. The title company's role is a very important process in the purchase transaction. They are responsible for checking that the title of the property is free and clear, and that there are no liens (unpaid debts) on the property. The title company will also make sure the closing statement (completion statement) is correct. The title company will send a copy of the closing statement to your agent before completion so that they can check it for errors.

It is important that your agent does see this form before completion to make sure your charges are correct. It has often been the case, when I have checked closing statements, that there have been errors resulting in the buyer being overcharged. Here again, your real estate agent can save you a great deal of money.

If you have a mortgage on the property be prepared to sign a large amount of documents pertaining to the mortgage from the bank. This is all normal and standard procedure.

At the completion, you will need to take a cashier's cheque (made payable to the title company) with the amount disclosed on the closing statement. This is for your deposit and completion charges.

A cashier's cheque is obtained from your US bank and is given as a preference to cash for large amounts over the counter. It is the equivalent to cash which means the title company can then release the keys to your new property to you or your management company immediately.

Alternatively, you can wire the funds directly to the title company if that is preferred. The title company then disburses all funds to the respective parties (seller, real estate agents, mortgage broker) at the end of the completion process.

19 THE COMPLETION (CLOSING) NOT IN ATTENDANCE (A MAIL AWAY)

This is by far the preferred chosen route for most buyers living overseas. A mail away is simply a completion by mail. The documents are sent to both parties through the post, signed and returned, by the date on the completion statement. There is a very strict time frame to this. **There is one task you need to do if you are not going to be present for the completion and that is to find a notary who is able to witness and sign the documents.**

This seems like such a small task yet it is one of the most overlooked aspects of the purchase process.

You will need to have your closing (completion) documents signed and witnessed by a notary when they arrive for you to sign.

There are a large number of documents to sign if a mortgage is involved. They are all standard documents that have to be signed to purchase a property. There are less documents to sign if you are making a cash purchase.

Sometimes you will find that your solicitor is a notary and is authorized to do this. Not all solicitors can perform this work. Make sure you check well in advance and have a notary in place. Your solicitor should be able to advise you of where to find the services of a notary if they are unable to do this themselves.

As soon as the closing statement and documents are delivered to you there is a strict time frame in which they have to be signed and returned. This is usually a matter of days and if you don't have your appointment already arranged with a notary the whole purchase could fall through.

Time is of the essence with the buying process and if you exceed the time limit for returning the documents then you will be out of contract. Do not let this happen to you. You could lose the property if the seller has a change of heart and this could give them the perfect opportunity to cancel the sale. Remember, this can happen so make sure you have made all the arrangements well in advance of the documents arriving.

Quick Tip

Check with your solicitor first as they may be able to recommend a notary. Your Realtor will check the closing statement for errors. Always ask questions if you have any uncertainty at all.

20 MANAGING THE PROPERTY FROM AFAR

This can be a lot easier than you probably imagine and it all boils down to two things.

1. Finding the right management company
2. Communication.

First of all the management company. They will give you a list of things you need to do before you can rent out your property. They will perform these tasks for you so there's no need to worry. They will look after maintenance issues, cleaning and dealing with guests. If you decide to rent out your property they may also provide you with bookings.

It may be more beneficial for you to rent out the property yourself if you are happy with spending time and effort on websites, marketing etc. However, if you don't have the time for this then the management company can usually do it for you.

Your real estate agent will have good contacts in this department as they will have firsthand knowledge of the way management company's deal with their clients. Always ask for testimonials from current clients so that you can be confident you are hiring a trustworthy, competent company.

Secondly, communication. Keep in regular contact with your management company via email, telephone and personal visits when you stay at your property. A professional management company will offer a website service and will keep you updated with your running costs and income on a regular basis.

Quick Tip

It is advisable to pay all of your utility bills to the companies providing the service by direct debit. This includes electricity, water, gas, telephone and cable TV. By paying your bills directly it will be easier for you to check the monthly charges are correct. Your management company can give you the relevant contact numbers to set up each service.

Always try to make things as simple as possible. If you pay your mortgage and bills from the same US bank account that you receive your rental income, this will make it much easier to manage your investment and save you a great deal of time and money in the long run.

21 RENTING THE PROPERTY OUT TO PROVIDE AN INCOME STREAM

It really depends on why you are buying a property in Florida. If you decide you do want to rent out the property then it is very important that you choose the correct management company that will assist with this. The company will take bookings, on your behalf, at a lower rate than you might achieve yourself, however, they will also relieve you of all of the advertising and marketing hassle.

Providing you have followed the advice above and purchased your property in the right location, there should be no difficulty in renting your home out.

It is very important that your house is decorated and furnished to the best standards for the rental market. It must have all of the necessary amenities that people require when taking a holiday to Florida. These include flat screen TV's, DVD players and DVD's, games room, pool towels and internet connection.

Your management company will give you a list of what is required to obtain the full potential in the rental market. If your house is of a more basic standard it will not be the first choice for someone making a booking.

Standards in Orlando, Florida are exceptionally high compared to many European destinations and people expect the best. If you get this right, your property will provide you with a stream of repeat bookings from people who have enjoyed the holiday of a lifetime.

For your peace of mind, you should ensure that a deposit is taken from your guests to cover any accidental damage that may be caused during their stay. Your management company will check the property on each departure to make sure it is in the same condition as it was before your guests arrived.

22 REPAIRS AND UPKEEP

Here is another reason why it is important that you employ a good management company. The company will regularly check the property for necessary repairs and for any cosmetic, decorative updates. You will be advised of the cost before the repair is done unless it is below a certain amount that you have previously agreed. In that case the management company will action the repair and invoice you for the amount. It is important that the property is kept in excellent working order and that repairs are undertaken quickly and professionally.

Expect to paint the property inside on a yearly or two yearly basis, depending on the number of bookings that are taken. Daily wear and tear can quickly make a beautiful property look shabby. Repairs are a normal part of owning a property and make sure you take this into account at the time of purchase.

23 TAX LIABILITIES

If you own a property in Florida, you will need to file a yearly tax return in the US. If you have received rental income this must be declared and the necessary expenses deducted. Certain deductions could include mortgage interest, repairs, annual inspection visits to the property and many more.

I would highly recommend that you employ the services of a good CPA (tax accountant) to make sure this is done correctly. There may also be certain expenses that you can deduct which you are unaware of. Your real estate agent will be able to recommend companies that can assist you with this. Again, make sure you ask for testimonials from existing clients.

Also, make sure your UK accountant is fully aware of your second property ownership and income. They will advise on the best way to document this for your annual tax return.

24 SELLING YOUR PROPERTY, SHORT SALES, FINANCIAL PROBLEMS

It is a buyer's market in Orlando at the moment and I would not recommend selling a property unless it is absolutely necessary. There are thousands of properties available with discounted prices of 40% - 50%.

If you absolutely must sell your property, the first action you need to take is to talk to a reputable Realtor. Go to www.housebuyorlando.com and complete the request form so that someone can contact you to advise you properly.

The first job for your Realtor will be to perform the research to present you with an approximate valuation of your property. They will look at all of the similar properties recently sold, under contract and on the market and will then discuss the correct price that you need to list your property to make sure you have a good chance of selling.

The process is quite straightforward if you do not have a mortgage on the property and the property can be easily marketed. When a suitable buyer is found a contract will be written. Once both parties have agreed on the price then the contract is signed. If the buyer is obtaining a mortgage, the process to completion takes approximately 6 - 8 weeks. If you are lucky enough to find a cash buyer the time frame could be a lot shorter.

During this time, a property inspection and a pest inspection may be carried out on behalf of the buyer. Under the terms of the contract, if you have agreed to any property repairs, these will need to be done on presentation of the home inspection report.

Your Realtor will assist with all aspects of the completion process. It is not necessary to be present for the completion as this can be done via mail away (post).

If you have a mortgage on the property and you find that the selling price is less than the outstanding mortgage this will present you with a number of options.

1. You can either list the property on the market and when it is sold bring the remaining amount to the table to pay off the mortgage.
2. If you do not have the additional funds needed to pay off the mortgage then you can contact the bank you have the mortgage with and ask for a hardship package to put the property on the market as a short sale. The bank will request various different documents to prove you are in financial difficulties at this stage. You should only consider doing this if you can no longer make your monthly mortgage payment. You will nominate your Realtor to liaise with your bank and the property will be put on the market in the usual way. When an offer is received, it will then be presented to the bank and negotiated by them in the usual way.

3. If you can no longer pay your mortgage, the last option is to allow your home to go into foreclosure or repossession. After a few months non-payment of the mortgage, your property will be taken back by the bank and will still have the outstanding mortgage debt on it.

Quick Tip

If you are looking at purchasing a short sale or bank owned property, then you must be aware, that even though the price will be lower for the property, it is a very difficult process to complete.

Properties of this kind have usually been left unattended for quite some time and may be in disrepair. There may also be outstanding debts on the property (such as property taxes) which the bank may charge you for in order to complete the sale.

Even though the price may be lower initially, it is often the case that these properties need to have money spent on them to bring them up to a livable standard.

The process of dealing with banks can be one of complete frustration and may take months of phone calls and documents before any progress is made. Often the sale will fall through and the whole process has to start again.

It could be more beneficial to purchase a property at a higher price from a seller/owner. This could actually save you money, and definitely time, in the long run.

25 SUMMARY

I hope you have learned a great deal from this book about buying property in Orlando, Florida. The information should have provided you with the knowledge you need to help you move forward with the process of purchasing (or selling) your Florida property.

If it is your dream to own a property in Florida then your dream can now be fulfilled. It really is an easy and enjoyable process, provided it is done correctly. Make sure you use this book as a reference, re-read it to really help you absorb the information.

It won't be long before you can be enjoying your own Florida property, relaxing beside the sparkling pool of your dream home in the sun.

If it's an investment property you want to own then what are you waiting for? Now is the time to purchase property in Florida!

Email us today and we will provide you with details of properties that meet your requirements on www.housebuyorlando.com. We will be delighted to answer any questions you may have about the content of this book and the purchasing process that you need to follow.

Make a start now and simply follow the steps that I have gone through.

Your Florida property is waiting!

TESTIMONIALS

If you like what you have read and would like to forward a testimonial please send it to paula@housebuyorlando.com.

Printed in Great Britain
by Amazon